Affective
Jacob's Ladder
Reading Comprehension Program
Advanced Reading Curriculum for Social and Emotional Learning

Student Workbook

Picture Books, Short Stories, and Media, Part II

Student Name: _____

Teacher: _____

Joyce VanTassel-Baska, Ed.D., and Tamra Stambaugh, Ph.D.

Affective Jacob's Ladder Reading Comprehension Program

Advanced Reading Curriculum for Social and Emotional Learning

Grade 3

Student Workbook
Picture Books, Short Stories, and Media, Part II

Joyce VanTassel-Baska, Ed.D., &
Tamra Stambaugh, Ph.D.

Prufrock Press Inc.
Waco, Texas

Copyright ©2020, Prufrock Press Inc.

Edited by Katy McDowall

Cover design by Allegra Denbo and layout design by Shelby Charette

ISBN-13: 978-1-64632-184-1

No part of this book may be reproduced, translated, stored in a retrieval system, or transmitted, in any form or by any means, electronic, mechanical, photocopying, microfilming, recording, or otherwise, without written permission from the publisher.

For more information about our copyright policy or to request reprint permissions, visit https://www.prufrock.com/permissions.aspx.

Printed in the United States of America.

At the time of this book's publication, all facts and figures cited are the most current available. All telephone numbers, addresses, and website URLs are accurate and active. All publications, organizations, websites, and other resources exist as described in the book, and all have been verified. The author and Prufrock Press Inc. make no warranty or guarantee concerning the information and materials given out by organizations or content found at websites, and we are not responsible for any changes that occur after this book's publication. If you find an error, please contact Prufrock Press Inc.

Prufrock Press Inc.
P.O. Box 8813
Waco, TX 76714-8813
Phone: (800) 998-2208
Fax: (800) 240-0333
http://www.prufrock.com

Table of Contents

Fishing With Sam 2

Snack Attack 7

After the Fall 10

The Dog and the Shadow 15

The Crow and the Pitcher 18

Fishing With Sam
By Atle S. Blakseth

View the short film entitled *Fishing With Sam* at https://www.youtube.com/watch?v=xMnx_3BC7EM.

FISHING WITH SAM

Facing Adversity and Challenges

F3 1. How did Sam face his challenge? Was Sam's response an appropriate one? Why or why not?

_____
_____
_____
_____
_____
_____

2. What lesson about facing challenges and teasing can we learn from this video? Make up a moral that you learned from the video, illustrate it, and share with your group.

_____
_____
_____
_____
_____
_____
_____
_____

Analyzing Adverse Situations and Conditions

F2 1. Why do you think Sam did not react negatively when the penguins were teasing him with the fish? What might have happened if he had fought back in the beginning?

_____
_____
_____
_____

2. Have you ever encountered a similar situation in your life? If so, how did you respond? In the future, how will you know when to stand up for yourself and when to ignore the behaviors of others?

_____
_____
_____
_____
_____
_____
_____

Recognizing Adversity and Challenge

F1 What was the main problem the bear (Sam) faced in the video? State the problem in a sentence or two.

_____
_____
_____
_____
_____
_____
_____

FISHING WITH SAM

Demonstrating High-Level Performance in a Given Area

L3 What character traits were most important for success, according to the video? Which character traits do you have that will allow for your success? Which character traits do you need to work on? Create a table to contrast each list. Analyze the differences you see. How will you work to improve?

Applying Learning to Practice

L2 What did Sam learn from the penguins? What did the penguins learn from Sam? How, at the end of the video, did each animal use their strengths to get food?

_____
_____
_____
_____
_____
_____
_____

Recognizing Internal and External Factors That Promote Talent Development

L1 What skills did each animal have? Create a 3-column chart with one column each for Sam, the seal, and the penguins. Create a list of character attributes or strengths for each. Then, be prepared to discuss which animal strengths are most similar to yours and why.

Sam	The Seal	The Penguins

Snack Attack
By Eduardo Verastegui

View the short film entitled *Snack Attack* at https://www.youtube.com/watch?v=38y_1EWIE9I.

SNACK ATTACK

Using Emotion

E3 The old lady used her frustration in a positive way to get the cookies but in a negative way when interacting with the boy. Explain how your emotions can be both good and bad. Create a list of things you can do when your emotions end up being a bad thing. Use the list from rung 2 to help you think of new ideas.

_____
_____
_____
_____
_____
_____
_____
_____

Expressing Emotion

E2 How might the old lady and the boy have expressed their emotions in a more positive way to solve the cookie problem? Make a list of possible responses. Illustrate your favorite response on a separate sheet of paper.

_____
_____
_____
_____
_____
_____
_____
_____

Understanding Emotion

E1 1. How did the old lady's assumptions about the boy impact her emotions and her response toward him?

_____
_____
_____
_____
_____
_____
_____
_____

2. Have there ever been times when emotions got in the way of your thinking and reasoning? How did you handle it? Did you behave more like the teenager or the old lady?

_____
_____
_____
_____
_____
_____
_____
_____

After the Fall
By Dan Santat

What happened after Humpty Dumpty's fall? Humpty Dumpty is now terrified of heights. How can he start doing things he loved again, like bird watching from high up on the city wall? How will he face his fears?

AFTER THE FALL

Facing Adversity and Challenges

F3 Humpty showed great courage in facing his fears. Describe a fear you have, and then explain something you did to overcome it. Create a T-chart that shows your fear in the first column and what you did to overcome it in the second column.

Analyzing Adverse Situations and Conditions

F2 Humpty said, "accidents happen." Yet Humpty was still afraid to retrieve his airplane, knowing another accident might occur and all the king's horses and all the king's men might need to put him together again. What made Humpty choose to climb the wall anyway?

Recognizing Adversity and Challenge

F1 Would you say Humpty's greatest challenge was: himself, his past negative experience, or the wall? Support your answer using evidence from the story.

_____
_____
_____
_____
_____
_____
_____

AFTER THE FALL

Engaging in Productive Risk-Taking

G3 Think about a decision you need to make. Create your own decision-making grid like you did for Humpty in the second rung. Add criteria that are important to you. Rank them. How might analyzing multiple options help you decide when or if to take a risk?

_____
_____
_____
_____
_____
_____
_____
_____

Considering Multiple Perspectives

G2 What factors did Humpty consider when making his decision? Think about the criteria from the story that were important to Humpty and how he viewed each. Some criteria have already been completed for you. Rate each criterion, according to Humpty. Then, add an importance total or weight based on Humpty's reaction. Review the chart and totals in the third column. According to the chart, should Humpty have climbed the wall? Explain.

_____
_____
_____
_____
_____
_____
_____
_____

Affective Jacob's Ladder Reading Comprehension Program: Grade 3, Picture Books, Short Stories, and Media

Question: Should Humpty climb the wall and risk falling again to pursue his goal?

Criteria or Factors Important to Humpty	Ranking (1 = not at all, 3 = somewhat, 5 = totally)	Importance/Weight (× 1 = not that important, × 2 = important, × 3 = very important)	Total Ranking × Weight
Safe but sometimes accidents happen			
Allows him to see birds and meet his goal			
Total			

Identifying and Calculating Risks

G1 What kept Humpty from reaching his goals and doing what he loved—watching birds? How did he compensate? Create a story board to show the problem and solution of the story.

_____
_____
_____
_____
_____
_____
_____

The Dog and the Shadow
By Aesop

A Dog, crossing a bridge over a stream with a piece of flesh in his mouth, saw his own shadow in the water and took it for that of another Dog, with a piece of meat double his own in size. He immediately let go of his own, and fiercely attacked the other Dog to get his larger piece from him. He thus lost both: that which he grasped at in the water, because it was a shadow; and his own, because the stream swept it away.

THE DOG AND THE SHADOW

Engaging in Productive Risk-Taking

G3 Analyze the following risks we often take in life. Identify potential benefits and losses for each.

Risk	Potential Benefits	Potential Losses
Not doing your homework		
Investing money in the stock market		
Dining out in a restaurant during a pandemic		

Which of these three scenarios carries the greatest benefits? Based on your chart, how would you describe your willingness to take risks on a scale of 1–5, 5 being high and 1 being low?

_____
_____
_____
_____
_____
_____
_____

Considering Multiple Perspectives

G2 Analyze the risks the dog takes. What are the perceived benefits of his going after the shadow's meat? What are the risks? Under what circumstances is such a risk worth it, do you think? What other factors would you want to consider, such as the size of the dog, your own strength in wrestling another dog, or other creatures who might intervene?

_____
_____
_____
_____
_____
_____
_____
_____

Identifying and Calculating Risks

G1 Write a moral for this fable about risk-taking. Explain it. Use a separate sheet of paper if needed.

_____
_____
_____
_____
_____
_____
_____
_____

The Crow and the Pitcher
By Aesop

A crow, dying of thirst, came upon a pitcher that once had been full of water. When the crow put his beak into the mouth of the pitcher, he found that only very little water was left in it, and he could not reach far enough to get at it. He tried and tried, but at last had to give up in despair.

Then a thought came to him. He took a pebble and dropped it into the pitcher. Then he took another pebble and dropped it into the pitcher. Then he took another pebble and dropped it into the pitcher. Then he took another pebble and dropped it into the pitcher. Then he took another pebble and dropped it into the pitcher. At last he saw the water rising toward him, and after casting a few more pebbles into the pitcher, he was able to drink and save his life.

THE CROW AND THE PITCHER

Facing Adversity and Challenges

F3 Create a chart, showing your responses to different challenges we may encounter in life. Two are listed below to get you started. Please identify three others on your own and cite your potential responses to them. Provide comments about your thinking.

Challenge	Response	Comment
You have limited resources for attending extracurricular activities and lessons.		
You become ill and miss 2 weeks of school.		

Analyzing Adverse Situations and Conditions

F2 What factors did the crow need to consider in his situation? Make a list of questions he needed to ask. Consider both internal and external factors.

_____
_____
_____
_____
_____
_____

Recognizing Adversity and Challenge

F1 How did the crow respond to adversity? What did he do first and then second? Make a flowchart of his actions. What would you have done differently? Why?

THE CROW AND THE PITCHER

Demonstrating High-Level Performance in a Given Area

L3 1. The crow's actions mimic those of a scientist. What aspects of the scientific process does he demonstrate? Describe as many of the following scientific research processes as you can.

Scientific Process	Crow's Action
Defines the problem	
Collects materials/data	
Makes a hypothesis	
Tests the hypothesis	
Draws a conclusion	
Replicates the experiment	

2. How does having a process to follow promote thinking in a field? Provide a one-paragraph response.

_____
_____
_____
_____
_____
_____

Applying Learning to Practice

L2 How do you solve problems? Write out the steps and skills you would use to solve the following kinds of problems:
- I have too much work to do and am falling behind in my studies.
- My parents blame me for disobeying them about going to bed late.
- My pet is making messes in the house.
- I do not have any close friends.

Recognizing Internal and External Factors That Promote Talent Development

L1 1. Create a fable, using animals of your choice, to show how a seed can change into a plant. Describe the process the animals employ to demonstrate that change. Use the following outline and the space below to organize your thoughts.
- Animals selected
- Outline of the process they go through
- Conclusion of the fable
- Moral

_____
_____
_____
_____
_____
_____
_____
_____

2. What factors help plant growth and development? What helps you grow and develop as a learner, do you think?

_____
_____
_____
_____
_____
_____
_____
_____

Please visit our website at
http://www.prufrock.com

Printed in the USA

$19.95 US